Amateurs at Love

For Julia –
and all her
creative
energy
xo
patricia.

AMATEURS AT LOVE

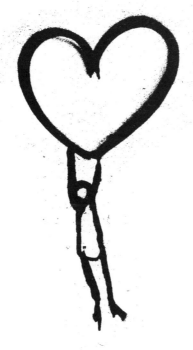

PATRICIA YOUNG

icehouse poetry

Edited by Anita Lahey.
Cover and page design by Julie Scriver.
Cover image: Nick Fewings, Unsplash.com.
Title font: Navy Queen One by Sean Cody, Vintage Type Company.
Printed in Canada.
10 9 8 7 6 5 4 3 2 1

Library and Archives Canada Cataloguing in Publication

Young, Patricia, 1954-
[Amateurs at love (2018)]
Amateurs at love / Patricia Young.

Poems.
ISBN 978-0-86492-991-4 (softcover)

I. Title. II. Title: Amateurs at love (2018)

PS8597.O67A72 2018   C811'.54   C2018-901166-1

We acknowledge the generous support of the Government of Canada,
the Canada Council for the Arts, and the Government of New Brunswick.

Goose Lane Editions
500 Beaverbrook Court, Suite 330
Fredericton, New Brunswick
CANADA E3B 5X4
www.gooselane.com

For LFC

THIS COULD BE
ANYONE'S STORY

WHAT DOES LOVE MEAN? the girl asked. The boy shook his head. They were sitting on the steps of the church with five green domes, passing a bottle of beer back and forth. Earlier a wedding party had poured like white foam through the arched doorway. Rice and confetti littered the steps. Well, what do you think it means? I think, he said, then paused to drink some beer...I think it means a boxcar going off the rails, grain spilling down a gully, fermenting over summer, a bear gorging on that grain, passing out in a field, a bear that could wake any moment, hungover and thirsty and ready to kill for a drop of water.

HE MADE A FETISH from a piece of ginger root and walked it back and forth across her stomach. A kid, she said, you're like a kid with a new toy. She was lying on a chaise longue in a mango bikini. Their couplings alternated between diffidence and passion and when they got drunk they didn't throw dishes. Would you like me better as a girl? he asked. An hour later: What kind of question is that? If this were a play, their dialogue would be described as intermittent. It would be called sparse. She would be *the girl* and he *the boy*. No one else would enter or leave the villa. Just one scene in a summer-long performance. And the chain-smoking director? In time, he would destroy them as he had destroyed all the other young lovers.

THE WOMAN STEPPED OFF THE BUS in a little blue dress and gladiator sandals, and then the man drove her to a bar where they ordered a bottle of wine. They talked about myth and tradition and the socialist dream. She said, I'm not crazy about Madrid, but Barcelona... The more they drank, the more prickly their talk. She accused him of conceit and idiotic theories. He reproached her for spreading rumours. An underage fugitive was *not* living in his basement. It was the same whenever they met, on whatever continent or rocky catamaran. For a moment they ceased bickering and listened to a strange chirring sound, like the sound of film rewinding in an old Polaroid. The camera clicked shut and their voices picked up again, growing so loud and quarrelsome that the waitress came over and asked them to move to a table outside. They laughed when the waitress mistook them for husband and wife. On the patio overlooking the sea, they ordered another bottle and continued to argue. They divorced and remarried three times that afternoon.

FOR HER NINETEENTH BIRTHDAY he gave her a suede belt from which metal leaves dangled. She thought a wife was someone who followed a book of recipes down a dog-eared path. But the path turned dusty. It grew quiet as sand. Sometimes the bread doesn't rise — the flour's too heavy, the yeast's too old — but when the fever passes you tie your hair back and scrub down the walls. Each morning before leaving for work he kissed her cheek while she slept, his steel-toed boots stepping through the tail end of dawn. She thought about that on the long afternoons she walked through the forest, feeling nothing, understanding nothing, the leaves around her waist like a string of silver bells.

EVERY MORNING OF HIS VACATION the boy ran ten kilometres into the desert, and later when the sun floated above the lake he bought blueberries and apples from Fernandes', a roadside shack spitting distance from the American border. An old man weighed the produce, then scrawled numbers on a piece of cardboard. In the middle of his calculations he'd look up, as though pleading with the boy, as though to say, What am I doing here? His granddaughters bustled around him, shucking corn, covering the fruit bins with wet blankets, serving pie and ice cream. The boy was in love with them all, especially the gap-toothed youngest who, on his last day, fixed her eyes on his. Never trust a rattler, she said. If you cut off its head, it can still bite.

SEX, HE SAYS, you'll like it. No, she won't. She's lying in a hammock strung between fruit trees. What makes you so sure? he says. My best friend's cousin's ex-babysitter. The summer issue of *Seventeen* is spread across her stomach. He's older, the son of her parents' new best friends. Back from Cuba, they're inside the house, crushing ice and muddling mint for a jug of mojitos. He opens his mouth to say something. Instead, gives the hammock a push. Every now and then another little push. Later, they'll walk down to the lake with rolled-up towels. They'll stand on the wharf and observe the turquoise pollen dusting the water's surface. He'll convince her to take off her suit and jump in. But right now, curled inside a string cocoon in the heat of the day, she feels inviolable. It will take forty years before she'll feel this way again.

IN THE SPRAWLING RUINS the students wander among the mosaics, guidebooks under their arms. The boy with a lazy eye says love is a complex emotion whereas lust is merely an element among other elements. The talk turns to their philosophy professor who for months insisted love was a mental condition to be cured like any other illness, but that was before she became obsessed with her sister's husband and climbed a ladder into the couple's bedroom. This fever has become an intolerable torment, she announced to the sleeping man and woman, then turned and climbed back down. But remember, the boy with the lazy eye says, our professor isn't young or old, blond or brunette, thin or voluptuous, she's an inflammable idea, a burning field of unrequited passion. The other students don't disagree. They just slough off their sweaters and pass through a narrow gate one at a time, smiling and murmuring in the brilliant sunshine.

IF HE HAS TO DIE he wants to be murdered by a jealous husband. He wants to be shot in the husband's bed, having just made love to his wife. The artist relays this fantasy to his adolescent model while painting her astride a child's hobby horse. Years later at a New Year's Eve party, he cuts in on another man's partner. Performing a drunken, tongue-in-cheek tango, he dies of a heart attack. The model, now middle-aged with several PhDs and marriages to her credit, is surprised to inherit his estate. She sells most of the canvases to collectors and galleries, keeping for herself only those on which her young body is displayed in various stages of undress. Not once in the years she modelled for him did he try to seduce her. But oh the look in her eyes.

AFTER CLASS SHE JOGS the wood-chip trail around the golf course. She's written her last exam and it's started to snow. On her final stretch three masked men — no, they're boys — step out of the bushes in front of her. Down on your knees, bitch, says the one with the knife. A fist slams into her stomach. She buckles. A palm mashes her face into sawdust and mud. Two boys take turns, first one, then the other, but the third says, No. What the fuck, says the one with the knife. No, the third one says again, and turns and lopes away. But he doesn't go alone. She leaps after him. Even as she lies bruised and bloody on the ground, even as his feet pound the wood-chip trail, she flies after him. No matter how fast he runs or how far he travels she is there, riding his heels: the stone in his shoe, stitch in his side, grit in his teeth. Large as a question and close as a lover, she follows the third one to the end of his days.

ALL MONTH THE HONEYMOON couple wakes to rain hitting the leaves outside their hotel window. Umbrellas bob along the sidewalks like strange black pods. On their last morning, eating breakfast beneath the portico, the couple glances up: a caravan of wild animals is rolling by. The giraffe stands perfectly still on its platform, head erect. The tiger paces its cage, the zebra's stripes dazzle. Zoo's drumming up business, the waiter says and pours more coffee. And the rain keeps falling on the weedy girls hawking flowers in the square, on the boys selling paper cones of pomegranate seeds. It falls on the elephant raising a listless trunk like a kid in a back seat, bored and asking: Are we there yet? Are we there?

IT WAS AFTER SHE LEFT. After she left *me*. It was after she confessed to peppering the burnt grass around the perimeter of the house to express her disappointment. Generally speaking, she was a disappointed woman. It was after she started wearing umber and rags, but before she dragged a loaded pistol back and forth across the lawn in a threatening manner. Did I say that? Did I say she threatened *me* with a pistol? It was after her failed public performance, but before her personality fragmented. She was what she was—awkward and jittery, indiscreet and scowling, a bracingly attractive woman in a crowded theatre lobby, sipping a glass of Chardonnay. It's three in the morning and I'm still awake. How could she leave me? How could she walk away until she was nothing but the sound of a shoe slapping against wet pavement?

THE NIGHTS WERE COLD, so he gave her one of his shirts to sleep in. It was made of Egyptian cotton. Neither of them knew: was it the beginning of something or the end? Lying in bed, he told her stories about his childhood in the Far East. He talked about love and longing and the endless possibilities but really, what did he say? One morning she woke to find him gone, his clothes and books, laptop and coffee mug. As though he'd never walked those slanting wood floors, flossing his teeth. Driving to the tennis courts, she hallucinated the brown hills undulating like camels' humps. For the next hour she slammed balls against the practice board until she realized she'd never see him again. This could be anyone's story: seven weeks in a house perched on the edge of a hillside, a man's voice breaking like a narcotic through a woman's skin.

MY HUSBAND'S MISSING ARM was a mystery. He never mentioned the lack of it and I was too polite to ask. Besides, he had balance. He had style. Once, he stepped onto a slack line strung between two trees, walked twenty metres before falling off. He taught life skills to young offenders. Drove delinquents around the neighbourhood in a beat-up van, looking for odd jobs: painting fences, raking leaves, digging up storm drains. My husband was tolerant of the boys' goof-ups and fist fights, their sudden outbursts and electric rage. He could slice bread, chop wood, and do one-arm push-ups as well as any man. But this isn't a story about overcoming obstacles. It's about his merry band of reprobates huddled outside a country church on the day of his funeral. It's about their scuffed boots and inscrutable faces.

IT'S AUTUMN WHEN HIS WIFE peers out from behind a dresser, sly, catlike, not more than sixteen the year she went to college: smart girl in the campus cafeteria dipping fries into gravy. He crawls across the floor, afraid a sudden movement will startle her, make her disappear. A ghost come back to haunt him? No, her appearance is more thoughtful than that, more indifferent. Sweetheart, he says, reaching out to touch her, but she's all business, estate lawyer and bank accounts, pension and life-insurance policy, details she hadn't time for during those last cadaverous months, wanting only binoculars to observe the songbirds outside the bedroom window. She nods toward the closet door. Inside there's a rack of woollen coats. Choose one, she says, urgent, fading, losing volume, but how can he choose? They are too many, too beautiful, coats the colour of gourds and squash, burnt orange pumpkins, coats buttoned with berries, wheat-stem collars, acorn-studded lapels, kale-leaf cuffs.

I STOPPED AT THE SIDE of the road and peered into an open workshop: dirty machinery, tools hanging on a wall, a twisted car radiator. A man wiping his hands on his overalls stepped out of the shadows. I went mad thinking about her with another man, he said, as though picking up on an earlier conversation. My love for that woman was a heavenly flame that gave light to the world. And then he swatted the naked toddler clinging to his pant leg. The child stumbled onto the road causing a bike-driven cart to swerve, spilling onions and eggplants. I rushed to pick her up. Who does she belong to, I said to the man, Is this child yours? He shrugged and I pushed the toddler into his arms and walked away, but she followed me along the canal, back to my hotel, through wind and fire, into sickness and old age, calling, always calling.

A WOMAN IN A LONG WHITE COAT is walking across a frozen lake toward the grand hotel on the opposite shore. Snow dusts the hills. The man waiting for her in a sixth-floor suite has been waiting for years, bread cooling on a board, wine uncorked. The temperature rises. Rain begins to fall. Eyes fixed on the hotel's tiny rectangles of light, the woman keeps walking. With each footstep her heart beats faster. Melting ice creaks beneath her weight. A chambermaid bearing fresh towels knocks on the man's door. A mist falls over the lake. Nothing is visible now — not the snow-dusted hills or the woman in the long white coat. What happens next? Does she sink below the horizon? Do the man and chambermaid marry the following summer beneath an airy tent? What kind of story is this anyway? Does the grand hotel endure?

BLACK VINES AND TURQUOISE FLOWERS. Sweet smoke rising from water pipes. Silhouetted figures gazing through portals. I was sitting on a corner bench of the tea house when the young widow appeared beneath an arch inscribed with arabesques. A string of dried cantaloupe seeds hung around her neck. Her features were blurred by grief and the smoke filling the room. I watched her wander as she wandered every night from table to table, finally stopping beside mine. May I? she said and squeezed in beside me. She leaned against the cushions and sighed. I want to sleep, she said, I want nothing but sleep; I want to sleep among the rustling stalks and slender pods and when I wake I want to hear him walking through the garden, saying something commonplace, saying, Pick the beans.

INSIDE SLEEP COUNTRY, BIRD MURALS glow on the walls: peacocks and flamingos, macaws and parrots. The old man wants a firm mattress. The old woman longs for a good night's rest. But the warehouse is a gruelling maze of daybeds, canopy beds, waterbeds, platform beds, sofa beds, truckle beds. Beds the size of coffins and sandboxes. Beds sluggish as tugboats and shallow as wading pools. They lean against a child's bunk and remove their shoes. After you, he says, and she begins her ascent. They climb the ladder, heads butting through clouds and sunsets, until they roll, exhausted, onto a super-deluxe, memory-foam mattress. Lying on their backs, they talk about old wounds, betrayals, and whiplash, lust and bursitis. They have children, don't they? Grandchildren, too? The lights dim. They hear the last customer leave. Doors lock. Plumage rustles. There's a lone *creeing* sound. They reach shyly across the expanse. After all these years, how is it possible? They're still amateurs at love.

THEY WALK TO THE STORE for a jar of sweet pickles, and when they return everything is gone. Damn, he says, I must have left the key in the door again. They walk through the empty rooms. Not a chair to sit on, not a spoon for soup. Walls bare of art, rugs rolled into thin air. Even the cake cooling on the counter has vanished. Only dustballs remain, cobwebs in high corners. They imagine the Queen Anne bed bought at an auction fifty years earlier riding the back of a pickup to LA. They push the windows open and there in the trees: children hanging like possums, dangling like caterpillars. *Their* children. The children she lost year after year in her monthly sheddings of blood. The earth shakes. Colour drains from the sky. Light becomes wind and wind becomes music. A Ukrainian polka? So this is what death feels like, they think, as the children take to the air, even the girl with the skeleton key clenched like a rose between her teeth.

"SPAIN IS
A STATE OF MIND"

—Patrick Friesen

.

Menorca #1

My husband and son are up to their necks
in the Mediterranean. First,

something about me. I am not wind-driven,
but the smell of ancient clay

is lodged in my brain. Any moment now
Odysseus et al. could sail around the corner,

rape and plunder on their minds.
So many steps, the girls coming up said

as we were going down. Last week,
squid carapaces washed up on shore:

stink of blue ink rimming the bay.
No one knows what to do

with a landscape like this
except bow down to the madness of God.

Within the hour the sun will slide
behind sandstone cliffs riddled with caves

in which Moors once hid from invading
Christians and Christians once murdered

the next army of unholy conquerors.
Unholy conquerors! Armies of

Christians once murdered other Christians,
then hid from invading Moors

behind sandstone cliffs riddled with caves.
Within the hour the sun will slide

down. When the madness of God bows
to a landscape like this

no one knows what to do.
A stink of blue ink rims the bay.

Squid carapaces wash up on shore.
Last week, as we were going down,

the girls coming up said, So many steps,
rape and plunder far from their minds.

Could Odysseus et al. sail around the corner
any moment now? Lodged in my brain

is the smell of ancient clay.
I am not wind-driven but something about me

is Mediterranean. First —
my husband and son ... up to their necks.

Barcelona

Can a man tipping his head, shaking the sea out of his ear,
still be a boy? It's always like this after he leaves.

The light dives underwater.
Because sea and sky are two shockingly different blues,

I keep watching for my lemon thief, my wild-garlic forager,
my cava-drinking boy to step off the horizon.

Ants are swarming again in their mighty thousands,
carting off flecks of the fig he squashed underfoot before he left.

Why, a friend asks, do we long for our sons when they're here,
right here in the room sitting beside us?

I imagine mine walking the Gothic Quarter,
his long, loping stride, dark glasses, and faded jeans.

My room's bigger this time, he writes
when he arrives at his cheap hotel. A balcony

overlooks an inner courtyard. In every doorway —
a girl who answers to the name *Malvina*.

Menorca #2

> *The palm at the end of the mind,*
> *Beyond the last thought, rises*
> *In the bronze décor*
> —Wallace Stevens, "Of Mere Being"

The wind gusts at the edges of our minds,
siliceous and traced with sandstone.
Slate and shale are omnipresent.

An olive tree bows in the wind
without fruit or longing.
Roots cling to shallow soil.

The island's at the mercy of unreason.
Its olive trees bend.
Leaves glisten.

Bronze stones moonscape the northernmost tip.
The *tramuntana* molds everything in its path.
The azure sky makes us neither happy nor unhappy.

Granada

On every street corner young men appear,
apparitions rising like steam from the pavement.

Closed black pods huddle at their feet.
So this is what happens when it rains in Granada:

on every street corner young men appear,

snapping umbrellas open.
Their oddly defiant act empties the mind.

Apparitions rise like steam from the pavement.

Three euros for a brief respite of shelter.
What future, what hope? Rain scratches at the church door.

On every street corner young men appear.

Already the clouds are breaking.
Already we're weighed down with regret.

Apparitions rise like steam from the pavement.
On every street corner young men appear.

Watching the Gypsy Boy Watch His Mother

Spain is a state of mind, you said, and rain falls mainly on the plain,
rarely on Sacromonte, warren of limestone caves
carved out of hard-packed hillsides. We'd come for flamenco,
whitewashed walls, and percussive footwork.

In Sacromonte, warren of limestone caves,
a woman stood at an entrance, erect and motionless.
Night dissolved into whitewashed walls and percussive footwork.
Can a floor be more than a floor? A dance more than a dance?

Erect and motionless, she stood at the entrance,
clicking her castanets. In Albaicínian operas
a floor is more than a floor, a dance more than a dance.
A son's love knows no bounds so who to watch, him or her,

clicking castanets. All through that Albaicínian opera
the *tocaores'* strummed, the boy's face
was love unbound. Who to watch, him or her —
Andalusian beauty strutting across the small stage?

I can still see the boy's face, hear the *tocaores* strumming.
For the finale she threw back her head and flicked her wrist,
Andalusian beauty strutting across a small stage.
Red dress, black lace, ruffled feathers. Her fan dropped open.

Where did we see a woman throw her head back and flick her wrist?
Up there, in the hard-packed hills, remember, flamenco,
red dress, black lace, ruffled feathers, a fan dropping open? Ah, yes,
you say, Spain is a state of mind and rain falls mainly on the plain.

ANIMAL TALES

It is impossible to sell animal stories...
> —from the rejection slip of George Orwell's
> *Animal Farm*

Cow

After her milk ran dry the old cow began to steal things — dipping tongs, rubber insole, a scrap of hemp rope. She also began to lie. One blowsy, spring evening, between mouthfuls of half-digested comfrey, she informed the other cows that she'd received a divine message: a violent quake would soon shake the earth on which they stood. Volcanoes would erupt. Cities would crumble. The barn's rafters would collapse on top of the animals as the ground opened beneath them. The other cows shifted their weight. They chewed their cud fretfully while the milk-dry cow whispered the terrifying details. No one will escape, she lowed in a hushed voice so as not to frighten the young ones, who, after all, were still trying to raise themselves up on wobbly legs.

Turkey

In the end, Buttercup, the most intelligent turkey in the valley, did not win the spelling bee championship. Up till then she'd won every bee she'd entered and in her short life she'd entered many. Buttercup was so dejected she didn't notice her boots were on backward, not to mention on the wrong feet. Failure made her anxious. She tried roosting in a nest threaded with larkspur and bergamot. Surely larkspur would calm her nerves and bergamot lift her spirits. While she fussed, her fellow turkeys strutted about, shaking their snoods and rattling their wattles. How absurdly pleased they were with themselves and yet not one of them had the mental stamina to memorize a word like *antediluvian*. Of course, Buttercup had spelled *that* word correctly. Having read widely, she was familiar with the era before the Biblical flood. She'd recited the letters of *antediluvian* without a glitch. No, Buttercup's downfall was *pococurante*, a word she ought to have known. Just look at them, a whole flock of layabouts bathing in dust. Complacent, she gobbled under her breath. Incurious. Indifferent. Nonchalant.

Rat

Percival, the circus rat, believed he was dead. He believed the lion had eaten him whole. No need to worry about me anymore, he said to his wife, I am consumed and deceased. Good God, she thought, I'm married to an idiot. She leaned down and bit her husband's tail, causing him to emit a high-pitched squeak. Ah ha! she said, a dead rat wouldn't squeak. Percival shrugged. Death doesn't trouble me, he said. Everyone knows a dead rat makes a superb trapeze artist. To prove his point, he scampered up a ladder after the big top had emptied and dangled from a rope clenched in his jaw. He began to spin in faster and faster circles. Even the lion watching from his cage understood: if you're dead, you're invincible. On the sawdust floor, beneath her husband's rotating body, Percival's wife stood on hind legs and held out her tiny paws. She knew it was useless. I am merely a spectator, she thought, I am not a net.

Rooster

Let us agree, the rooster said to his favourite hen, that life on a farm is idyllic and cruel. Let us scuttle through our daily run with lyric arrogance. What purpose to our existence if not to animate the Earth? Outside this coop, light hurts our eyes, but let us agree that the sun riding high above the trees looks benevolently down upon us. With our aerodynamic dreams and uncertain futures, let us scatter our droppings across this straw floor. It's true that once I crowed such an improbable tale that it found its way into the *Book of Gallinaceous History*. Sin and pride hang on a shoestring, but when the coop door springs open and we hustle through the tall grass, oh my love, the world will hear such hackled joy.

Horse

Whoa, the horse thought, after consuming a bucket of fermented daisies. Up till then he'd spent his days galloping through the countryside, across streams and over hedges, occasionally rising up on hind legs and neighing for the sheer joy of being a horse. Now he stood in the same corner of the paddock every day, blinking his butterfly lashes. What's wrong with that horse? the other animals asked. Is he sick or just tired of life? They didn't understand that the horse could now see heaven and hell, the power and glory, the unfolding universe, the great and small: tumbleweed, for instance, caught in posts and ditches, hopscotching across the prairie, snagging on barbed-wire fences, wheels of tumbleweed rolling across the land like sun-scorched angels.

Dog

Every morning the blue-eyed dog with the lopsided tail ran down to the river to splash about with the other dogs, all of them yelping and snapping at each other's haunches. It was a shallow, meandering river until the day in November when rain fell so hard and fast that the river rose quickly and burst its banks. The dogs scattered and ran home, all except the blue-eyed dog with the lopsided tail.

The dog's master, a boy of ten, liked to tell fantastic stories to his younger siblings before bed, but now debris dammed his imagination. Every plot turned tragic. Every character a drowned dog or inconsolable boy. In time, the river receded, revealing the muddy corpses of bicycles and turntables, plastic basins and deflated tires. And then one night in early spring, long after the boy had given up hope, a camas bulb appeared in the sky like a swollen moon.

Goat

An old man searching for his goat came upon a whistling salal bush whereupon he collapsed in a fever and dreamt a bittersweet dream in which a girl from a bygone era kissed him on the mouth. He woke just in time to see a cougar crouching on the branch of a nearby tree. Before the man could think, the big cat leapt upon him, tooth and claw. Already depressed and thus preternaturally fearless, he wrestled the cougar to the ground, prying its jaws open, but there was no trace of goat blood on the cat's breath. The cougar fled and the old man sat on a rock and buried his head in his hands. He wept until nightfall and he was still weeping when the sun rose to a familiar tinkling. He looked up and, lo, his beloved pet was trotting toward him, the bell around her neck now three silver coins. After that, who could say who led whom down through the hills and into the field of blazing sunflowers?

Lamb

It was March and hyacinths blanketed the hills. For weeks the girl
had slept rough, on the hard ground. Some people hear the word
lamb and think mint sauce, an earthy Syrah. Not the girl. She wasn't
a shepherdess, nothing as pastoral as that, but to her, the lamb was
like a child — *her child*. She held the warm, bleating creature in her
arms, cooing and rocking and singing songs. One evening down
at the creek's edge, beating her undergarments against a rock, she
looked up and saw the lamb's mother charging toward her. The
full force of the ewe knocked the girl into a parsnip bed. Each time
she tried to pull herself up, the ewe knocked her down again. The
lamb, watching from a distance, grew bored and wandered away.
For several years he gambolled along the border of one country and
another, finally stopping in a village of melancholic artists who took
to painting the lamb or fashioning his head in clay. Sitting for a
particularly morose sculptor, the lamb grew nostalgic and decided
to return to the place of his birth. The next morning, he set out
retracing his steps and after many wrong turns arrived at the hills
blanketed with hyacinths and parsnips growing along the creek's
edges. And there they were, the ewe and girl, still locked in battle,
still bleating at each other like bunchberry rams.

Rabbit

When the children peered through gaps in the fence surrounding their play area they were confronted with a shocking sight — a teenage girl whipping a rabbit with a willow branch. The girl heard the children's whimpering and came over and threatened to whip them too. So young and so pitiless, the daycare workers said as they shuffled the little ones into the church basement where they sloughed off their Muddy Buddies and rolled out their mats. It was time to nap. Time to dream. That night the children told their parents about the girl and rabbit, and the next day their parents told their friends, who then told their friends, and so on, person to person, until rumours of the girl's pathology travelled around the globe, full circle, returning to the rabbit who merely rolled his pink eyes. The children were fantasists, of course. To the rabbit's mind, truth was the water dish in the corner of his hutch, the whiff of clover on a summer morning, the diamond stud in the girl's ski jump nose.

Mouse

Before dawn the pregnant mouse ventured out of her hole in the abandoned lace factory and discovered pea-soup fog. Earth had dissolved into sky and sky had dissolved into earth. The mouse climbed onto her bike and pedalled toward the big house where, she knew, toast crumbs would soon be falling from the breakfast table. For the first time in her life she found herself travelling out in the open without a morsel of fear. The fog was so thick she couldn't see her nose twitching in front of her face. Surely no predator, not even those with elliptical vision, could pierce this rare autumnal shroud. She yodelled with gusto as she passed the empty loading bays, so taken with her own brazenness that she didn't notice a paw reach out of the mist and swipe her bike wheel. She flew over the handlebars, somersaulted in the air, and vanished in the miasma. Thereafter, generations of mice who lived and died among the hushed looms and silent shuttles would listen in wonder to the tale of the audacious mouse and her unborn litter.

Pig

The bride and groom paddled toward a small island off the coast, heading straight for the point of a desolate isthmus. The couple had been planning this wilderness honeymoon for years, since the day they met at a Polish deli where, at separate tables, they'd both ordered pork-stuffed cabbage rolls. The bride felt a shadow fall over her body. A miniature black pig was flying above her left shoulder. She raised her paddle to swat the ungainly creature, but he continued to hover menacingly. As the pig swung low, the groom shouted from the rear, Duck! He unintentionally smacked his beloved on the side of the head, stunning her into unconsciousness. When she came to, the groom was pulling the canoe onto the pebbly beach. He was making soft grunting sounds and the pig, balanced on an arbutus branch, was licking salt from his rose-petal wings.

Goose

The goose was in love with three ganders and they loved her in
return. The farmer, however, had no time for romance. Financially,
he was in over his head and also underwater. He needed to
downsize. This worried the animals, especially the goose. A month
earlier, on her birthday, she'd laid her last egg. Now, no matter
how she bore down — not one speckled oval. Like all lovesick
creatures, the ganders were a font of ideas and suggested the goose
feign broodiness. An excellent plan, she said, and refused to leave
her nest, even to eat or drink. Day and night her adoring ganders
gathered around to recite sonnets in praise of her fertility but after
the third debt collector had driven off, the farmer summoned his
hapless waterfowl. You've laid more eggs than any other goose, he
said, and I am grateful, but you are old, old girl, and now you must
return to the bee balm and sky. Too dignified to make a fuss, the
goose arranged her head on the chopping block and the axe came
down. Instead of blood, a bouquet of dandelions spouted from her
neck. The awestruck ganders watched as the yellow clusters turned
swiftly to seed balls. Puff, they cackled, puff, puff.

Duck

The old men didn't know the duck was a duck. Afflicted with cataracts and glaucoma, they assumed she was just another remote-control boat puttering around the pond across from their retirement home. The men operated their toys — miniature replicas of Second World War ships — from the sidelines, manoeuvring them around lily pads and torpedoes, plastic cups and enemy submarines. If the duck wasn't paying attention she might collide with a U-boat or bump beak to wayward prow. Day after day she paddled in leisurely circles, invisible to the men manipulating their controls and singing the heart-swelling songs they once sang in raucous dance halls. Only the very young with diamond-sharp eyes could perceive the duck's downy plumage as she crossed the shallow waters mined with devil's bit and wild iris.

Cat

When the house cat announced he was allergic to mould and dust mites and off-gassing plastics the barn cats laughed and accused him of hypochondria. I'm too weak to raid robins' nests, the house cat said, I vomit up fluff balls. What more proof do you need? He worried obsessively about his illness and began to wear a gas mask, convinced that toxic fumes permeated the air. Soon he was the butt of every farmyard joke. It wasn't just the barn cats. The raccoons hanging around the compost joined in, their hisses rising to a sarcastic pitch. Only the homeless tabby offered a sympathetic ear. Sidling up to the house cat, she espoused the many virtues of sleeping al fresco. Feel my pelt, she said, purring deep in her throat. Thick. Luxurious. Which is how the bedtime ritual began, the house cat standing at the side of the road around seven thirty every evening, hitching a ride to the nearby woods where he bedded down among the bittercress and chocolate lilies.

Chicken

A chicken in a velvet jacket festooned with plastic buttons appeared in the man and woman's bedroom around three a.m. They were reading and talking and flicking channels on TV. Lifelong insomniacs, they'd met in a chat room in the wee hours of the morning, desperate for conversation on the subject of mid-twentieth-century British cars — Rovers, GMs and Morris Oxfords. Such a happy coincidence to discover they were both sexually aroused by the smell of old leather seats. Look, a chicken, the woman said, stating the obvious. The man reached under the bed for his pellet gun, but just at that moment the chicken jumped onto the quilt and began to dance. The chicken's dance was so brash and ludicrous that the couple couldn't help laughing. They laughed and laughed, until their laughter opened up airways and arteries and blood surged through their veins. Soon the couple fell into an exhausted, subterranean sleep. When they woke the following afternoon, more refreshed than they'd felt in years, the chicken was perched on a bedpost. Follow me, she clucked, to a place where fireweed burns like a magenta sea...

Donkey

The orphan donkey longed for a family, a real family, not a mish-mash of quackers and mooers and honkers. One Saturday morning, pulling her vegetable cart to town, she imagined an array of relatives — practical jokers and sourpusses, skeptics and smart alecks, the grizzled and dewy-eyed, those in straw hats who lived in a fragrant state of grace. She imagined them clip-clopping alongside her, past stalks of swaying goldenrod. She imagined the members of her family in such intense and lively detail that by the time she reached the market, the farmer and cart had vanished and she'd entered a world in which only jacks and jennies existed. A shiver rippled up through her fetlocks. She closed her eyes (weddings and births, hee-hawing and accordion music, coloured ribbons and bales of sweet hay!), content at last, and when she opened them the sky had darkened and thousands of donkeys were snorting and pawing the ground. In an instant, she'd fallen in love, birthed countless foals, grown old, and died. A multitude of donkeys, more than the shooting stars growing in the oak forest, had travelled long distances to attend her funeral. She began to count heads but there were too many...donkeys...donkeys...all twitching their withers and swishing their tails.

PANGRAMIC LOVE SONGS

The Quick Brown Fox Jumps Over the Lazy Dog

The day you trip in and out of focus behind thick
glass I feel a **quick** jolt and then a pint-sized pilot's

skidding past in a **brown** raincoat. White horses graze
beyond the terminal. A **fox** pokes its snout out of my

suitcase. The omnivorous animal **jumps** off the conveyer
belt and into my arms. I've told you **over** and over

how jet lag blurs and slows the world down. By **the**
baggage claim, I hear someone say, Buck up, **lazy** girl,

it's all gonna be good. That's when I see you, **dog**-
tired and unshaven, hair electric, standing on end.

Frolic Pretty Wag-Lambs, Don't Quack XX At the Zoo-Jove

Frolic for God's sake, this isn't Versailles. Sweetheart,
you're too **pretty** for the guillotine. Surrender to the grass.

Wag your hips. Why the pierced navel and snakeskin boots?
Lamb among **lambs,** you're an eighteenth-century vision and I

too old for your beauty. **Don't** wrinkle your nose, girl,
don't stare at your feet. **Quack** for the hell of it.

Bleat for joy. Desire's seedy underside? **XX**-rated videos?
Banish the thought! Love's not a piece of stale cake.

At least, I assume explicit emperor/empress sex is not
the sort of flick you like to watch after a visit to the city

zoo: pandas and pythons, ice-cream and mini-train. By **jove,**
Antoinette, that was a day for the gods. Wasn't that a day?

Crazy Fredrick Bought Many Very Exquisite Opal Jewels

Crazy & soaring like Chagall's baker — that's you
Fredrick, body unbound. Gravity couldn't hold you.

Back then I **bought** into your horseplay on train
tracks, so why'd you leave me **many** years ago,

a barefoot sandwich girl? I'm still waiting to land
very suddenly on the roof, waving to the crowd.

Exquisite bridegroom, your left eye was a
common blue **opal.** Such a fashionista, trussed

up in leather and burlap. And **jewels?** Bring me
jewels, Fredrick, the way my father brought bread.

Quick Zephyrs Blow, Vexing Daft Jim

Quick! Morning kisses, mint tea, a swim across the lake,
gentle **zephyr's** wind: tail end of a hurricane. **Blow**

the goose shit off the wharf, you adorable **vexing**
man, can't you see I'm smitten, I'm dope-fiend **daft.**

Sun and rain and refracted light. Let's span the spectrum,
oh **Jim,** above your head, look, a prism arcs its rainbow back.

Pack My Box with Five Dozen Liquor Jugs

Pack me in your Roy Rogers lunch bucket, take
me to the beach. All **my** life I've been the sand

sucked beneath an outgoing tide. **Box** me up.
Wrap me in wax paper. **With** or without you

I take three steps forward, **five** steps back.
I'm staring down your childhood, I'm a **dozen**

brown eyes. Mother-Mother-May-I stir this cherry
red **liquor?** Rip off my mask and I'm an old-fashioned

cowgirl with a frosty glass **jug**, your Dale Evans
sweetheart warbling the happy trail blues.

My Girl Wove Six Dozen Plaid Jackets Before She Quit

My God, spiky vines attacked from all sides.
Last weekend a **girl** lovely as summer said,

Wanna pick some berries? Then **wove** her
gumboots through a field of cow plops **six**

centimetres deep. Here? I said. Here? Thorn
and thicket and three **dozen** skunk cabbages.

The air was sourly aromatic. In jeans and **plaid**
shirt she disappeared into the brambly mash,

hair a hive of yellow **jackets.** All morning
we snipped clumps of clotted fruit with secateurs

before I realized: I was torn, I was bloody.
Turning, I saw **she** was unscathed though prickles

crowned her head. Let's **quit** now, she said
and held up her bucket, brimming black jewels.

Farmer Jack Realized That Big Yellow Quilts Were Expensive

Farmer is as farmer was, I said, meaning our marriage
was a mess, **Jack**, a mess of broken tractor parts

we could not repair. Who **realized** first — a mad
beast was stalking our hearts? **That** month in Kenya

we hauled ourselves up just to teeter on the brink.
Big sadness, vast sky, doomed expedition. Ostriches

dashed across the **yellow** savannah — downy
feathers and flat heads. The earth was a gold **quilt**

rolling beneath their thundering feet. Those flightless
birds **were** as clumsy and elegant as the words

we could not utter. How **expensive** was that safari?
You held the purse strings. I drank like the damned.

Waltz, Nymph, for Quick Jigs Vex Bud

Waltz her deep into the sea where against
all odds light begins. **Nymph** she is not, nor

cheap sex logo **for** hire. Hair fringed in coral,
she stole your laptop, wallet, eyesight, plot.

Quick, Loosejaw, who's the true monster, the one
who kicks up a few **jigs** or the one who kills

for love? The ocean rises. No time to **vex** or
dupe with jacks up your sleeve. Tonight she glows

like a bioluminescent **bud.** Regard the queen of
darkness, her long thin fingers dealing black hearts.

How Razorback Jumping Frogs Can Level
Six Piqued Gymnasts

How broken the once-green world.
How peopled with **razorback** lunatics

slurping water like cacti. These days
we're all **jumping** shard-toothed fences,

landing on our backs. When three-headed
frogs appeared in the pond I phoned the only

scientist I knew: **Can** you identify the poison?
She happened to be my ex. Okay, I said,

level with me. Oh, no, she said, you step off
the bridge, plunge **six** hundred metres. How

lethal she'd grown. How deformed and **piqued**
after the divorce. And the kids? They could

become **gymnasts** for all she cared. Or prophets
walking ass-backward on toxic water.

Sixty Zippers Were Quickly Picked from the Woven Jute Bag

Sixty good years he gave me before his brain turned
to Swiss cheese. **Zippers** he also clasp-locked before

Velcro or Squeegees **were** invented. He licked salt
off crackers. Peeled grapefruit in bed. **Quickly** ate

the sections. My husband was as sane as the surf
until I **picked** out the first deranged thread.

Too late. He'd already passed **from** Lost to Vacant
to Boy Scout Glee. Those psychedelic years,

the seventies, remember, we hallucinated in polyester
suits. **Woven** the translation, he whispers, button

the gathers, **jute** the vowels. His velveteen mind swings
like a Seagram's **bag** full of marbles and hot, white stones.

FAMILY ALBUM

Mother

I took her hand and pulled her toward the park and begged her to explain why everything I wanted to know was unknowable, like the boys hanging around the edge of the canal. I wanted to know the difference between hypocrisy and lust. Also: the true story of Adam and Eve. Was the Garden of Eden a foreign country where you drank from a porcelain fountain or was it the beast with two backs? I wanted to know: how could a beast *have* two backs? Other things too: tricks to stay sane in prison. Should I memorize passages from the Bible or Dante? Hanging upside down on the monkey bars, I wanted to know why she, my mother, sitting on a stone bench unwrapping a small meat pie, had blotted out her past. She bit into the cold pastry, gravy oozing from the corners of her mouth, and I wanted to know, would I too have to reinvent myself with duct tape and flowers?

Brother

Demise, I whispered to my brother as I passed him on the landing. Demise, demise, demise. You've got weak knees, I said at dinner, Your death is imminent. That spring, fuzzy black-and-gold caterpillars dropped from silk tents draped between the branches of the crabapple trees on the boulevard. There is no afterlife, I said as he drifted off in the attic room where we lay feet to feet in a narrow bed. For dust thou art and unto dust shalt thou return. I loved my brother so much I reminded him each night that the caterpillars with white dots between their eyes were marked with death. Each morning I cupped his face in my hands and kissed his forehead.

Sister

She prayed to snow demons and communed with ice gods. Feet strapped into skis, she launched into orbit. If she broke bones, they were interesting bones. If she broke teeth, she shattered the archetypes. If she spoke in clichés, those clichés proved the universal truths. The difference between then and now is the shape of a triangle. I am speaking from memory, of the manner in which my sister flew down mountains, the cold wind lashing her face. In the end, she plunged back to Earth and entered the realm of myth. These days she's learning to sit up again. She's learning to talk. Sun, she says. Wings. Wax.

Husband

Last night I found myself at a kitchen party on the other side of the blue bridge talking to a boy in red cowboy boots. Beer bottles in hand, we walked through the French doors into a forest of oyamel trees. A full moon rose. I'd always wanted to visit a butterfly sanctuary in the mountains and now, incredibly, there I was. Monarchs alighted on our arms and heads and shoulders. For the next three hours we stood side by side in silence, listening to the whir of wings, and then people were putting on coats, our hosts were kissing their guests' cheeks: goodbye, goodbye. The boy and I turned to each other — this was it? We clasped hands like old lovers who understood they'd never meet again. I knew then I'd marry him. *Whoosh* ... I was out the door and in my car, driving across the rusting metal girders spanning the harbour, chanting as a child will chant: blue bridge, red boots, yellow moon.

Grandfather

Every spring he tore up the grass in front of his house, then lay down squares of antiseptic turf the way he laid ceramic tiles on his kitchen floor. A sodbuster's love song to my grandmother who sat for hours on the lawn, legs splayed, plucking out blades of flowering rye. If she's not happy this time, he'd say, I'm pouring cement. Their house is gone now and the lot is an empty field of grass doing what grass does — growing, flowering, turning brown, dying. But I remember the night my grandmother rose from the ground like a prehistoric bird and shook herself off. For a long moment she stood on the flat, green expanse looking up at my grandfather looking back at her through the bay window. The air was thick with wild seed. Drugstore tweezers dangled at the end of her arm like an ancient claw.

Grandmother

Once a week I slept over and we gabbed like girlfriends in her double bed, marathon chats into the wee hours. *What's the point of suffering? Are we alone in the universe? Is there a God?* Sometimes we talked about my grandfather, who died of mysterious complications related to his appendix. There'll never be another man as decent and handsome, my grandmother would say. Though he could be stern, a little controlling (there was a kite, *her* kite, a birthday gift, my grandfather struggling with the flying line, running above the cliffs, not sharing, not letting her hold the spool). She snored like a rusty elevator but I slept through it, a kind of white noise, like the hum of an old fridge or the fan spinning close to my head on hot summer nights. Her snoring soothed me the way waves soothe other people. Or wind. Or falling rain.

Cousin

Lexi possessed a larynx that could not be dismissed, showed up blond and stayed late, belted "Me and Bobby Magee" into a plastic shoehorn. Danced in front of a cheval mirror in fuck-me pumps. Could turn herself inside-out, a full-throated whirligig, no illusion of bawdy, but bawdy itself, the full range of striptease. A woozy drunk just like her father, pulled her jeans, clown-like, up to her chin.

Daughter

My daughter was leaning over a picnic table, drawing another primitive figure when a blackbird appeared above her head. Round bodies, stick arms, tiny bowling-ball heads. I stood beneath a willow's canopy watching the blackbird watch my daughter. She never bothered with eyes or mouths, fingers or toes. But navels! She ground a black hole through the centre of each belly. When she tired of human shapes, she ran over to the swings and pumped her legs, singing, *A coo fell offa, a coo fell offa, a coo fell offa dyke.* I was so entranced by her song, the way it weaved green and gold through the tree's pendant branches, that I didn't notice two boys slide off the teeter-totter and creep toward her scrapbook. Didn't hear their cruel laughter or see the blackbird swoop down and carry them off in its orange beak.

Husband

He grew up in a blue room by the sea, the light so hard and luminous it ricocheted off the walls. No books or toys in that room, no games or stuffed animals. Not even a make-believe friend. There was a telescope, though, a gift from an aunt. He spent hours gazing at meteor showers and constellations, globular clusters and planetary nebulas. A miniature peeping Tom, he spied through the windows of houses on the other side of the bay. Parents just like his own were going through the motions, their lives as kaput as the wringer washer behind the kitchen door. How that clapboard house shook when he jumped on his bed, his father at the bottom stair, shouting, I'm going to tan that kid's hide, while across the bay, other boys in other blue rooms were also bouncing on lunar rilles, tumbling headlong into lava craters.

Son

That spring he and his friend rushed through the front door every day after school. With the care and single-mindedness of furniture movers, they'd push back couches and chairs, remove vases and lamps, wrap the milkmaid figurine inside a dishcloth. I'd watch them make a space to get down and rumble, knowing that any moment they might drop their arm chokes and leg locks and return the furniture and ornaments to their original places. In the kitchen they'd spread peanut butter on toast and gulp down juice. Rush out the door, skateboards flying off curbs and plywood ramps. That spring, standing on the threshold between one room and another, I watched two boys grapple on a faded carpet with such ferocity they might have been falling into love's wild and tender death grip.

Daughter

She'd perch on a stool in front of the kitchen window leaking morning light, while I dipped my fingers into a cup of water and divided her hair into two thick chunks. She'd flinch at the cold drops falling on her neck, the too-tight braids. But all this changed the morning of her thirteenth birthday when a little bald man arrived at the back door wearing a tool belt and carrying a suitcase of props. For two hours he built my daughter's hair up with blocks and balloons, straw and chicken wire, Styrofoam and netting. Later, in the village, she ignored the gawkers staring and pointing at the lacquered shell balanced on top of her head. My daughter walked so slowly and with such grace she might have been moving underwater, and when I looked again she *was* underwater. Down there, strands of hair loosened and swayed like sea grass. Her arms webbed into fins. Her brain shrank. Gill respiration expanded. Ears disappeared. Legs melded into a single flipper. People gathered round: Is this something new, they asked. Is this the evolutionary process in reverse?

Son

My son and I entered the last room together. It smelled of pipe tobacco and sunlight and ancient books disintegrating like old lace in your hands. What first appeared a mystery turned out to be God, a florid man with bulging cheeks. His crown was too big for his head and he wore his robe like tragedy. Purple fruit dropped from branches. I was tired of symbols. Tired of gods and tragedy and purple fruit. My son, meditating cross-legged on the floor, opened his eyes. Why are we still here, he asked, when everything's happening on the other side of the mountain? And then he smiled to himself. Such a stupid question. He'd always known his mother had no answers.

Aunt

I saw a child turning cartwheels on the lawn, my aunt searching for a fountain pen that came apart in four expanding parts. I saw the moon, a slice of lemon peel, lying on its back. I found the pen in a hair salon, propped up in a jar of turquoise disinfectant along with combs and brushes, all four parts expanding. And then my aunt was driving off in a convertible, the top down, her perfect updo blowing apart. I called after her — Your pen, your pen! — but she was already sealed with a seal that could not be broken. The child was on her lap and they were heading for death. I know the devil's in the details but I also know what I saw: a '64 Galaxie sprouting spangled wings.

Mother

All winter she texted me from beyond the grave. In life we had little to say to each other but now we couldn't stop. Thumbs tapping madly, messages flying back and forth, day and night hundreds of truncated missives ending in terms of endearment. It seemed we were both crazy for the same things: kelp skirts, fish-scale leggings, black nail polish, octopus earrings, dolphin violins. By the time the poppies drooped their floppy heads, my mother had become land and water to me, clownfish and guinea fowl. She was the meat I tore out of a crab's leg, the wine I gulped down in thirsty mouthfuls.

Family

We meet in a bombed-out villa, chandeliers missing bulbs, broken clerestory windows. The walls are threadbare curtains that don't reach the floor. But none of this matters because we're together, all of us sitting on church pews on either side of a long table. Someone's brought a pot of okra stew. Someone else has brought bread. My parents are here as well as aunts and uncles, the estranged and those living in foreign countries. Also cousins I've never met. Our tribe reunited at last, talking and eating and laughing until my father notices there is no wine. I look down the table. He's right, the glasses are empty. I'll go buy a few bottles, he says. No, I say, you're my guest but he gets up anyway. Then I'll go with you, I say, and I do, and so there is wine.

Father

My father is doing something complicated with a vise and hammer
and tiny nails. Is he a carpenter? A sandal maker? There's a knock
on the door. Is it a life-or-death knock? Two men in coonskin caps
are standing on the porch. Why have they arrived at my childhood
home in coonskin caps? Is this my childhood home? If so, where's
the farmhouse surrounded by fruit trees? Where's the tetherball
and rope swing? And why do the men look like my father? Are
they my father split into different selves? Does my father *have*
different selves? And then I'm on the Eurostar, entering the tunnel
without a passport or destination. As the train emerges into light
I remember that I left my father rolling a cigarette in the kitchen
without saying goodbye. I left all three fathers. I have always been
careless with people and now it's too late.

IMPERFECT VILLANELLES

Dream of the Newborn

Over breakfast I hold onto the dream,
revisiting it again and again,

especially the part where I bathed and swaddled the baby.
Later, stepping through the garden ravaged by storms,

I hold onto the dream. Over breakfast

I remember the child's mouth rooting round,
latching on, the familiar tugging sensation.

Again and again I revisit

the sting of the let-down reflex. And then I remember
that I remembered I was no longer young.

Over breakfast I hold onto the dream in which

I looked down at the baby, so new and fierce and hungry.
Let there be milk, let the milk come, I said

again and again the morning I revisited
a dream over breakfast. It was all I could do to hold on.

The End of Poetry

When an elephant climbs down through a hole in the clouds
you understand the world will never be the same.

Don't look now but he's circling the bed.
Reach out, touch his rough hide.

The elephant climbs down through a hole in the clouds,

reciting poetry. A lifespan of three hundred years
and he's still talking about the blood of mulberries.

Will the world ever be the same? You understand

he was conceived on turbulent waters and born
in silvery grief. Admit it, you've come to the end of things

and the elephant climbing down through a hole in the clouds

is lost in a low-frequency cry. The earth rumbles
and he's gone, left for a place without words.

The world he doesn't understand will never be the same
now a hole has opened in the clouds. Look — an elephant
    climbing down.

The Angels in Hell

We admire the fallen ones—
their modesty and catlike vigilance.

Stripped of their status and wristwatches
they look like beekeepers or amorphous beings.

The fallen ones also admire

us, the shiftless and doleful, the ne'er-do-well.
Without them we'd shine less brightly.

Vigilant as cats overcome with modesty,

they tilt their heads to the traffic above,
bend to gather the hems of their grubby robes.

We admire the fallen ones,

those barefoot insomniacs who pace the unquiet hours —
singed wings and hair salted with ash.

So modest. So vigilant. Like cats
we admire those who have fallen.

Winter

The concession stand slouches at the edge of the lake,
windows boarded up, plywood warped and rattling.

Pink paint flakes like dry skin. Small birds peck
at candy wrappers blowing against its foundations.

At the lake's edge, a concession stand slouches.

Winter karate-chops the waves. The days
grow short, our shadows long, the last leaves fall.

Boarded-up windows. Warped plywood. Our rattling bones.

Geese wing across the sky. The locals have flown south too,
Arizona or Mexico. Turkey vultures hunch in bare trees.

The concession stand slouches at the edge of the lake

and the sign on every door: Closed for the Season.
How long since we said anything provocative?

Bored, we rattle like windows and warp like plywood.
We stand. We slouch. At the edge of the lake, we concede.

French Maid

I've lost my umph, the girl doll says. How did it happen?
Her fishnet stockings bunch around her ankles,

her feather duster's worn down to the nub.
In bed the boy doll senses something missing.

How did it happen, he wonders. How did she lose her umph?

She is missing, the fibre-filled girl who once bulged at the seams.
She grows weaker. Can't sit or stand or hold up her head.

Her fishnet stockings bunch around her ankles.

The boy doll carries her out to the garden and kneels beside her.
Lifts her wrists to examine the stitches under her armpits.

You've lost your umph, he says, how did it happen?

He runs his fingers through her scalp, untangles floss hair.
Searches for a leak, a microscopic tear, gently

unbunches the fishnet stockings around her ankles.
How did it happen? Why did this girl lose her umph?

Mice

They left in June, simply vacated the premises. *Premises?*
What kind of word is that? The wrong word, surely,

too grand for this shack in the woods. December now
and the table on the porch sags in the middle.

Why'd those turd droppers and soap eaters leave in June?

Maple leaves stick like starfish to the windows. We add
more wood to the stove, drink the good wine, then bad.

Bad? What kind of word is that? The correct word, surely.

For years we've tried to trap and outwit them. Now silence
behind the walls. Night falls, moonless. Of their own accord

those wily nest builders vacated the premises. Last June,

drunk on light, we heard torch songs wafting
heartbreak through five-hundred-year-old trees.

Heartbreak? What kind of word is that? A sad word, surely.
Who vacated the premises? The mice. In June they up and left.

Acknowledgements

I would like to thank the editors of the journals and anthologies in which some of these poems have been published: *ARC*, *CV2*, *Dalhousie Review*, *Event*, *Fiddlehead*, *Grain*, *Malahat Review*, *New Quarterly*, *Room*, and *Rusty Toque*.

"What Does Love Mean?" was published in *The Wild Weathers: A Gathering of Love Poems*, ed. Ursula Vaira (Lantsville, BC: Leaf Press, 2013).

"After Class She Jogs" (appearing as "The Third One") was published in *Kwe: Standing With Our Sisters*, ed. Joseph Boyden (Toronto: Penguin Canada, 2014).

"Menorca #1" was published in *In Fine Form: A Contemporary Look at Canadian Form Poetry*, eds. Kate Braid and Sandy Shreve (2nd ed. Halfmoon Bay, BC: Caitlin Press, 2017)

A selection from "Family Album" won Grit Lit's chapbook contest.

A selection from "Animal Tales" placed second in *Grain*'s Short Fiction Contest.

A selection of the poems from "This Could Be Anyone's Story" was a finalist for the CBC Literary Competition and published in a JackPine Press book (with Dorothy Field, artist and collaborator). Some of the poems from this section were also published in a limited-edition chapbook with Alfred Gustav Press.

"Pangramic Love Songs" was published on *Dragnet*'s online magazine, and also in its print anthology: *Dragnet Anthology 1*.

"Spain Is a State of Mind" was published as a limited-edition holm with Alfred Gustav Press.

"Husband" (p. 81) and "My Husband's Missing Arm" were published in *Consider the Paragliders*, a Baseline Press chapbook.

I would also like to thank my wonderful editor, Anita Lahey, for her enthusiasm, kindness, and keen perceptive eye. Thanks also to the members of my writing groups. Their raucous but astute feedback was always welcome.

I am deeply grateful to copy editor Amber McMillan as well as all the people at Goose Lane Editions who were involved in the production of this book: Susanne Alexander, Jeff Arbeau, Ross Leckie, Julie Scriver, and Alan Sheppard.

My enormous thanks to the Canada Council and the BC Arts Council for their support while writing these poems.

Photo: Claudia Haagen

Patricia Young is the author of twelve poetry
collections and one book of short fiction. Her poems
have been widely anthologized and also appeared in
six chapbooks and numerous magazines and journals.
She has twice been nominated for the Governor General's
Award for poetry and has won the Pat Lowther Memorial
Award, the Dorothy Livesay Poetry Prize, the CBC Poetry
Prize, the Bliss Carman Poetry Award, the Confederation
Poets Prize, and several National Magazine Awards.
She lives in Victoria.